How to: **Foam Free,** Festive Winter Floral

CW01647708

First Published in Britain 2023
Author: Gill McGregor
Designs by: Gill McGregor

Published by: Gill McGregor College Publishers
ISBN 978-0-9929332-5-8
Printed in the UK
Layout design: www.gillmcgregor.com

Introduction

Gill McGregor

The Festive season is a time for giving and sharing.

Showcasing nature's beauty for all to see.
As floral artists it provides the opportunity for us to adorn our homes, our cosy refuge, with flora, glitter and a little bit of glamour to evoke our emotions and enhance our surroundings.

The presence of flowers is known to improve our well being, providing an element of calm and relaxation in our hectic and sometimes stressful everyday lives.

The giving of flowers always concludes with a smile. A positive response which elevates the mood, reduces stress, lowers one's blood pressure and lifts one's spirit.

This foam free flower arranging book showcases a range of different Festive and Winter design styles and techniques using alternative mechanics which enable flora to last longer than those arranged in floral foam. Thus increasing the pleasure and enjoyment flowers bring to; the recipient, the floral connoisseur or your target audience.

I do hope you, like me, will enjoy exploring these design ideas, working with a variety of diverse mediums to arrange and display your festive décor and floral gifts.

Festive Greetings to all.

Precision cut Rosa "Lemon finesse" enhanced with gold glitter fronds create a super Festive design showcasing the Aspidistra and cone mechanics as an intricate part of the design.

This alternative mechanic is made from knotted and looped Aspidistra, wired fir cones and a length of plumbing pipe.

First introduced in "How to... Alternative Mechanics for Foam Free Floral Designs Volume 2" this mechanic has been further developed to consist of a concentric ring of 7 looped Aspidistra which lay flat against the rim of the vase by incorporating wired fir cones to assist support, control and anchorage of plant materials.

Aspidistra Knots and Loops,

P6

1/ Cut a 14cm length of 40mm diameter PVC push fit waste pipe. (Used by the trade for bath and sink waste.)

1/

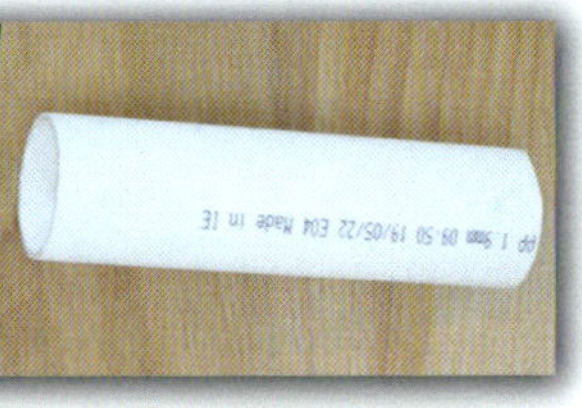

2/ Select 7 Aspidistra which are of like size. In turn make a loop and secure with green paper covered wire.

2/

3/ With 4 Aspidistra, manipulate each to form a knot. (The Aspidistra Knotting technique can be found on pages 70-73 of this book).

1cm Down from the top of the pipe, tape around the pipe using 12mm green pot tape. Position and secure your first Aspidistra knot at the leaf base to the pipe, where the circle of pot tape is already in position to aid adherence. Then tape the stem to the pipe at the base, making sure the stem is vertical. Repeat by placing the second Aspidistra knot directly opposite the first knot and secure into position, both at the top and bottom of the pipe.

3/

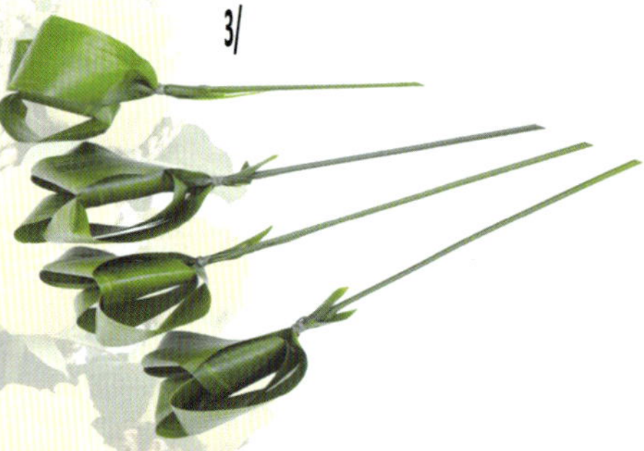

4/ Secure the remaining 2 knots to the pipe, with pot tape, in each of the spaces. You will find the aperture of the pipe is hidden by the fullness of the knots. The stems of which will extend beyond the pipe and act like stilts to assist water availability for the plant material arranged in the pipe.

4/

5/ Wire sufficient fir cones to make a concentric ring using green coated 30cm x 1.00mm wires and secure into position with pot tape. Ensure the cones are visible beyond the Aspidistra knots and are equidistant apart. Not only do they add a Festive feel but their weight will push down on the looped Aspidistra to make the loops splay out horizontally.

5/

6/ Push down on each of the 7 Aspidistra loops to help create a slight curve. Take the first loop and push it up towards a knot/fir cone, which will make the loop become more horizontal. Secure into position with pot tape at the top of the waste pipe. Repeat with the remaining 6 Aspidistra loops, ensuring they are equidistant apart to form a concentric collar. Complete by securing the stems of the looped Aspidistra to the base of the pipe with pot tape, so they too are vertical stilts.

6/

Select your vase and cut the Aspidistra stems straight across so they are long enough to rest on the base, inside the vase, and to enable the looped collar to sit on the rim. The stems beyond the pipe act as stilts and allow stems to go through at a diagonal angle to help hold your arranged materials to stay in position.

7/ The arrangement has been turned to showcase profile.

Remember when arranging the design the tallest placements must be able to touch the inside base of the vase and be arranged through the waste pipe. To measure the correct height needed for each placement, turn the head of the flower vertically, upside down, so as to gently touch your workstation so that you can gauge how tall to cut the stem straight across.

Arrange through the plumbing pipe first until full and stable. Finish by arranging through the Aspidistra knots, in between the fir cones and Aspidistra loops until you have completed your design for effect.

8/ If you are a Floral Art Demonstrator, you can remove the entire design out of the vase and tie into position with jute string to give away.

Woven Flat Midelino Ring

1/

For an extra long lasting design, why not enhance potted Poinsettias with a woven ring of wood band or Flat Midelino framed with a concentric ring of Picea pungens (Blue Pine).

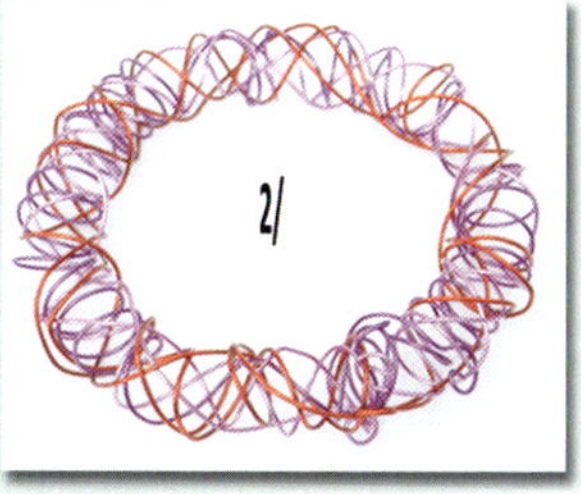

2/

1/ To create the Woven Flat Midelino Ring a 41cm (16 inch) flat wire ring was taped with green tape before Flat Midelino was, randomly, woven around and through the wire ring, secured with metallic wire.

2/ A coiled aluminium ring was made, as the mechanic, to fit around the potted Poinsettias to support the arranged concentric ring of precision cut Blue Pine.

3/ The design was finished by placing the Woven Flat Midelino Ring on top of the base Blue Pine. Additional Blue Pine was then arranged through the Midelino structure to hold it into position and for effect.

3/

No water was put into the silver metal container, as Poinsettias do not enjoy sitting in water and the Blue Pine can dry without its needles dropping. Water the Poinsettia plants as required.

Fir Cone Rings

P10

Using fir cone rings provides a wealth of uses, with or without supporting arms, for your floral décor.

To make, select a 31cm (12 inch) flat wire ring. Tape all parts of the ring with brown florist tape to both disguise the ring, as it will oxidize, and to provide some textural integrity. If you require arms for the ring to sit diagonally above a vase, tape individually, 2 x 50cm x 1.8mm Stub Wires and then tape to the ring on opposite sides to act as supporting arms.

Select the same sized fir cones and insert one at a time into the ring and screw the base of the cone between the outer rings to secure into position. Repeat the process making sure the cones are firmly anchored whilst locking together and hiding the inner struts.

Within minutes you have a circular fir cone ring.

For this hand tied of Rosa "Avalanche" positioned diagonally in a globe vase for effect, trails of Hedera (ivy) have been led from the hand tied and wound around the fir cone ring to assist the ring staying in place and to provide unity.

Fir Cone Rings

A fir cone ring with supporting arms has been used to enhance this simple vertical design of Rosa "Avalanche" using a soft bottle shaped mesh of Aluminium wire as the mechanic.

All plant material is precision cut, with the stems resting on the inside base of the vase.

A simple shallow dish houses an Aluminium wire domed circle using the Alternate Chain Link Technique, as the mechanic. (Featured in How to Floral Foam Free Volume One) A concentric ring of Picea pungens (Blue Pine) was arranged through the domed mechanic. The fir cone ring has been placed on top and additional Blue Pine has been arranged between the cones to help hold it into position. Finally a few bracts of the Poinsettia have been arranged centrally for that Festive feel.

Salim Triangle

P12

Having purchased this Salim pyramid, I decided to use one side and stitch a chain of threaded snowballs around the outer edge for effect. I then manipulated the triangle into a Hogarth curve shape and opened up the Salim to enable the structure to sit securely on the outer rim of my elegant grey vase.

Using 1 bunch of 20 Dianthus “Moon Aqua“.

I took 4 strong, straight stemmed Dianthus and arranged in the hand to form a dome and secured by banding with pink aluminium wire.

Circa 10cms down from the top grouping, I created a second concentric ring of 5 Dianthus secured with banded aluminium wire. Each time creating additional aluminium coils for visual effect.

The process was again repeated using 6 Dianthus.

The grouped structure was then placed into the vase. 3 Fatsia japonica leaves were arranged to hide the aperture before arranging a concentric ring of 5 large Dianthus at the base. A snowball was pinned to each grouping for effect. The design was finished with 3 individual Aluminium coils which veiled the Fatsia and were graduated in size, to assist unity.

Aluminium Star Alternate Chain Link

P14

Using one packet of 2mm x 100g Aluminium wire bend at 2cms before measuring 10 x 10cms lengths to make a zigzag shape. Do not cut the wire.

Manipulate into a star shape. Do not cut the wire.

Uniformly wind the aluminium wire tightly around the wire star shape to create a strong outline. Do not cut the wire.

To create the alternate chain link mechanic, use the remaining wire. Commence by wrapping the wire around a 1.5mm plastic test tube to create a circle shape, slip the wire off the test tube and repeat in the opposite direction to create a long chain of circles, equidistant apart.

Commence wrapping the alternate chain link around a star point until softly covered and then lead the chain across to a different star point and repeat. Complete by using all the alternate chain link to create a visually balanced covered star. Curve the star points for greater interest.

Repeat to make a second star with a second full packet of 2mmx 100g aluminium wire.

With a third packet of aluminium wire, make an alternate chain link measuring 40cms which has a straight 10cm length of aluminium wire at each end.

Mechanic - Interconnected Table Design

Using half a bunch of Liriope gigantea (Lily Grass), secure with an elastic band and insert through the centre of a star to create a short handle. Divide the half bunch by 6. Weave randomly, 2 or 4 grasses (dependent upon the number of blades in half a bunch) through each star point. Ensure you achieve visual balance. You will have 2 or 5 blades remaining that are protruding from the centre. Repeat the weaving technique with the second star using the remaining half bunch of Lily grass.
Place each star to rest on your chosen vase/ glass with the elastic banded grass sitting in water. Stage on a suitable base for effect. Interconnect the 2 stars with the 40cms aluminium alternate chain link. Weave the protruding Lily grass through the chain for effect.

Finish with a bunch of 10 short Rosa, arrange 7 through one star mechanic and 3 in the other. I added a small amount of Osmanthus heterophyllus (Variegated False Holly) for that Festive feel.

Mossing a Circular Wire Ring

1 - Use a 31cm (12 inch) flat wire ring, secure mossing twine to the inner ring and take 2 handfuls of teased moss; unwanted items, insects and creatures removed.

2 - Roll the teased moss into a firm 'sausage' shape.

3 - Place the 'sausage' shaped moss on to the ring. Lift the ring up to bring the mossing twine from underneath the ring towards you.

4 - Wind the twine over the moss towards the void & lift up the ring to bring the twine towards you from underneath. Tug to secure.
Repeat every 3cms. (1 inch)

5 - Take 2 more teased handfuls of moss & roll to create a firm sausage shape and push up against the previous sausage and bind securely to the ring.

6 - Continue to make additional firm moss sausages & bind onto the wreath ring securely.

7 - Repeat, making sure the moss sausages are firm, not too thick and cover the ring.

8 - Finish by making a moss sausage the size to fit firmly between the bound sausages to complete a solid moss ring and secure by binding.

9 - To 'cast off', make a loop with the twine and then lead the ball of twine through the loop and pull to make a knot. Cut the twine and insert the end through a bound twine placement.

10 - Trim the moss to make a neat and even mossed ring.

Your foundation is now complete ready to make your door wreath.

Basing a Mossed Ring with Picea pungens ...

P18

Using a mossed 31cm (12 inch) flat wire ring, bind to secure a 20cm (8 inch) flat wire ring onto the upper surface so that part of the ring can be seen inside the larger mossed ring. Plait 3 lengths of 60cm (24 inch) jute string and place around the ring and tie the ends together to form a "hanging loop". Take a small piece of string and tie the loop as near to the mossed ring to stop the loop from moving. Screw in 6 identical sized fir cones into the 20cm ring, making sure they are secure.

Prepare the basing by taking 2 large branches of Picea pungens (Blue Pine) and cut down to make 3 different length piles. Cut the larger lengths to circa 20 x 18cm (7 inch) "hand sized" bushy tips, then cut around 25 x 14cm (5 ½ inch) " 3 pronged" tips and then 30 x 6cm (3 inch) tips.

To base the ring, cast on by tying the jute string onto a side of the ring (not at the top or bottom). Begin to base (cover) the 31cm mossed ring by placing a 14cm "3 pronged" tip diagonally against the outer side of the wreath so the tip touches your work bench and the stem end is on the upper surface of the moss and position a 6cm tip - pointing the same way on the inside of the mossed ring and bind to secure with the string. This is called edging.

Repeat edging once or twice more so that the lengths of pine are in close, neat order to hide the sides of the mossed ring. Each time try and pull the string through the needles so when bound tightly the string cannot be seen amongst the pine.

Take an 18cm "hand sized" length of Blue Pine and place on the upper surface to hide the remaining top surface moss and bind so you cannot see the string.

Then repeat by edging the outer and inner rings as before until you can see that an 18cm "hand sized" frond will hide the top surface. Continue this process until you have based the entire ring.

Finish by completing the fir cone circle with 6 more wired fir cones and add further decorative items for effect.

When inserting wires into the moss make sure they do not come through the back of the moss – otherwise the wires will scratch your door. It is better to insert the wires at an acute diagonal angle into the moss and then face (position) your materials upright or as desired.

This wreath will need to be positioned in a sheltered place as if the cones get wet they will close and fall out of the wire ring.

Bauble Collar Table Design Using the . . .

P20

Making a bauble collar provides such a festive feel for your floral designs. I find it easier to commence making this design as a hand tied making sure the first placements are in the centre and then to complete the design as an arrangement.

To make the wire chain twist mechanic.

Cut 5.25 metres of rustic wire. Measure 2.625 metres, do not cut. From that measured point commence wrapping the wire around a rolling pin measuring 4.5cms in diameter. Make one wire cross over the other tightly and turn the rolling pin 360 degrees to create a double twist. Slip out the rolling pin. Do not cut the wire. Repeat making the adjacent twist in line with the previous twist.

Repeat to make 12 circles. Do not cut the wire.

2/ Join the 12 circles together by binding tightly one of the wires around the first circle and the last circle.

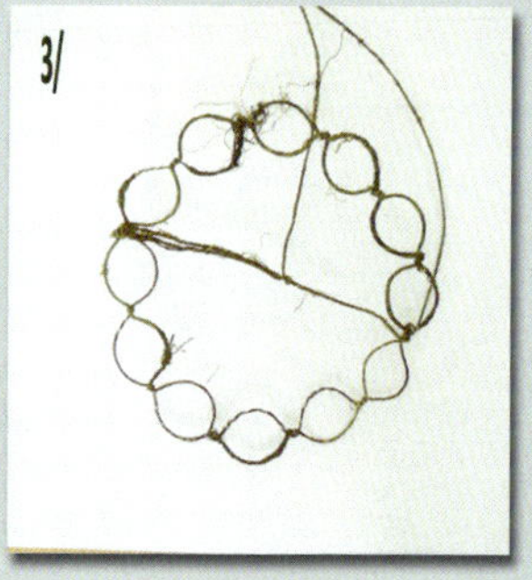

3/ Start to make spokes which are two circles apart.

Take one wire and lead all the way across and wind around the twisted wire so there are 6 circles either side. Lead the wire to the centre of the straight wire and twist in the middle.

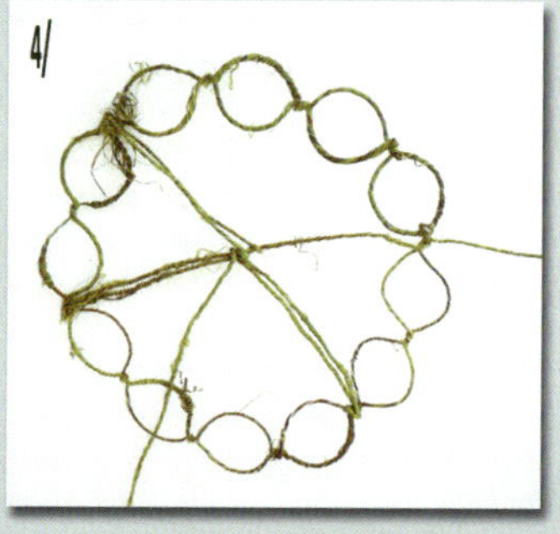

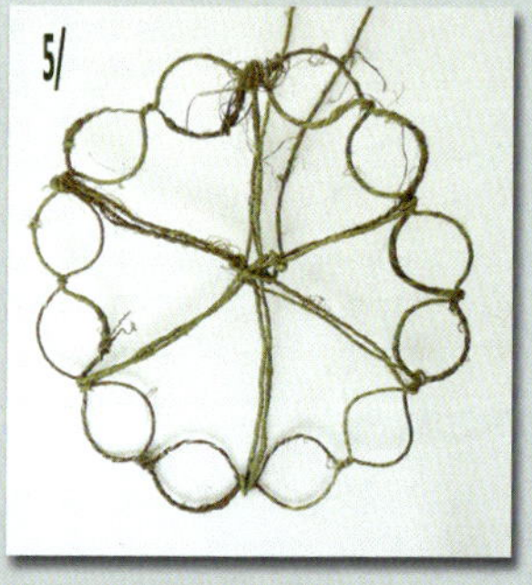

Wire Chain Twist Technique

4/ Lead the wire to a twisted wire 2 circles away from the previous spoke, twist around the double twist and then lead the wire to the centre and secure with a twist.

5/ Continue using the other length of wire to make 6 spokes which have 2 wires each and lead the residue wires to the centre.

6/ Make 3 double lengths to form a handle and wind the remaining wire to make 2 loops. For a hand tied the wires are close together to form a handle. For an arrangement they are open, to help stems be inserted through.
Pull out the spokes to make a diamond pattern.

7/ To attach the 12 baubles to the wire chain twist mechanic, cast on with a length of paper covered wire. With the upper surface of the mechanic facing you, insert a bauble through a chain hole and thread the bauble with the paper covered wire before binding the wire around an adjacent twisted rustic wire. Do not cut the paper covered wire , bind around the rustic wire to you reach the next hole.
Take a second bauble and repeat the process.
Continue to repeat this technique.

8/ Finish attaching 12 baubles.
They will be wobbly but don't worry.

Bauble Collar Table Design Using the . . .

P22

1/ Insert through the bauble structure your central Rose and 5 stems of Hypericum. Stems parallel. Tie into position with jute string.

Cut the string.

2/ Select your vase and cut the stems to size so that the structure sits diagonally.

3/ Arrange 6 roses to create a slightly domed shape. Each stem is inserted through a rustic diamond.

4/ Arrange foliage between each bauble to hold the baubles into position.

5/ You will find the centre of the arrangement will be nearer to the centre of the vase when more materials are added.

Finish by adding 7 identical looped Aspidistra, Eryngium and Pine for effect.

Alternatively, you can create the chain twist mechanic using Aluminium wire and thread soft tulle through the loops before making a posy arrangement in the same manner.

Interconnected Red Star Mechanic ...

P24

When using an Aluminium mechanic in the vase and a decorative Aluminium mechanic on the rim of the vase, prevents the necessity of using foliage to hold the flowers in place.
A lovely design which definitely evidences "Less is more".

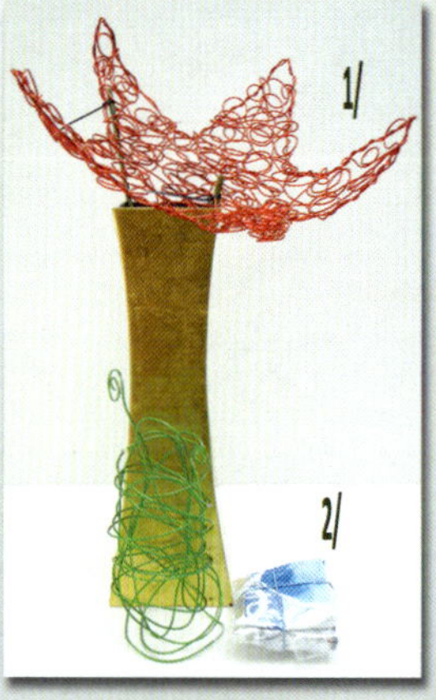

1/ Using the alternate chain link technique to make an Aluminium star mechanic (see page 14) a larger star can be made. You will need to use 1.5 packets of 2mm x 100g Aluminium wire to make this star with the points measuring 15cms and the test tube of a diameter of 2cms to make a slightly larger circle chain.

2/ I placed a bundle of sterilised cellophane held in place with rubber bands to sit in the base of the vase to reduce the need of extra long stems.

3/ Aluminium wire was wound around an empty wine bottle to create a light mesh, as a second mechanic, to arrange my flowers through.

4/ The ends of the wire are both at the top and coiled so they can clip over the edge of the vase to hold it into position.

5/ Push the light mesh down into the vase and clip into position.

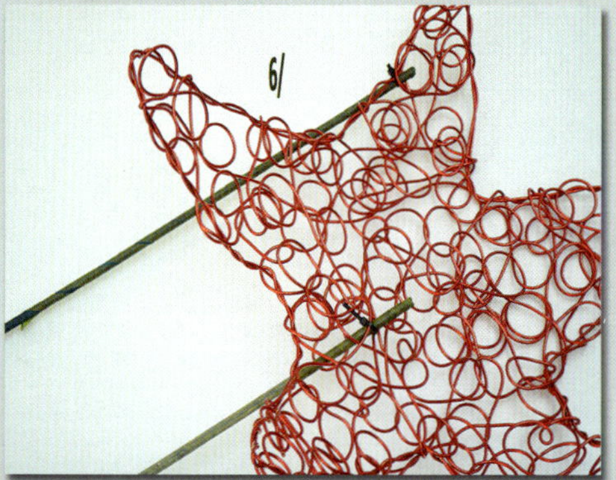

6/ Attach 2 taped orchid sticks using thin cable ties to the star. Cut the sticks to your desired length, so they rest on the inside base of the vase to enable the star to be arranged so it sits diagonally for effect. Fill the vase with water.

7/ To achieve the correct visual height you may need to pot tape 2 Rose stems together. Do make sure the end of the tallest stem is still able to have sufficient water in your selected vase.

8/ Arrange the design, emphasising the use of space.

No foliage has been used to showcase the transparent star.

9/ Finish with an interconnected star (its points measure 7cms in length) resting on a small glass vase with one complementary Rose and glittered placement.

Aspidistra Rose

P26

1/ Grade in size 5 Aspidistra leaves.
Have green paper covered wire ready.

2/ Using the smallest leaf, hold the leaf at the leaf base- upper surface facing you and manipulate the leaf so that the midrib vein is at right angles to the stem.

3/ Begin to twist in the leaf.

4/ Then fold the leaf blade away from you to make a flat top and continue to twist the leaf towards you.

5/ *Continued from 4/*

6/ Continue to twist the leaf blade and fold the leaf away from you, every now again, to create the centre of the rose.

7/ Gradually you will have twisted the leaf to form a tight centre.

8/ When you have circa 10cms of leaf tip remaining, fold away from you and secure the tip tightly at the leaf base.
Do not cut the wire.

9/ Take the next smallest leaf and hold its stem next to the "rose" centre. Fold the leaf away from you before commencing twisting towards you to increase the size of your "rose".

10/ Continue to fold the leaf away from you to make a flat topped rose whist twisting.

11/ When only the 10cm tip of the second leaf is remaining, secure with the paper covered wire.
Do not cut the wire.

12/ Continue using the third largest leaf. Hold next to the "rose", fold the leaf away from you and twist.

13/ When you have used up all the leaf by folding away from you and twisting, secure into position with the paper covered wire. Do not cut wire.

14/ Add the fourth leaf and repeat the technique of folding and twisting.

15/ You will find that you will be folding and twisting the leaf less as the "rose" increases in size. Once the tip of the leaf is only remaining bind the wire to secure. Do not cut the wire.

Aspidistra Rose

This simple design incorporates sculptured Asparagus virgatus (Tree fern) to frame the Aspidistra "Rose".

Small groupings of Pinus add textural contrast against the Fatsia japonica leaves for effect. A few gold baubles complete the design to match the bound gold metallic wire.

16/ Finish the "rose" with the last leaf, repeating the technique and secure into position with the wire.

16/

Plaited Palm Structure

P30

The curved line of plaited Kentia palms showcases rhythmic movement in this design. Red and green are Festive favourites and what better way to use exotic Anthurium "tropical" bracts contrasting against transparent plaited structures to evidence a complimentary colour harmony.

The palms will dry in a warm room environment without spoiling their plaited shape. Just make sure they are secured tightly to allow for both the stems and the fronds shrinking due to dehydration over time.

3 x 100cm Kentia palms have been plaited, to form the basic structure of this free standing design.

I selected a shallow red dish, a screw driftwood base, a dismantled red bath puff and manufactured striped candy canes and a pin holder as the main mechanic and accessories.

Having removed the base of the hollow cane, I wrapped some paper towel and 12mm pot tape around the screw of the driftwood base (or you could use a protruding long screw in a pre cut base) and pushed the cane down onto the screw for support and placed the mechanic into the dish.

A pin holder was then placed in the shallow container to anchor the limited flowers and foliage used.

The plaited palms were strategically attached for effect by securing with white Dacron string bound and tied as tightly as possible.

The design was then arranged with some of the Anthuriums threaded through the plaited palms to aid stability before being firmly pushed onto the pin holder. Festive red baubles, Fatsia leaves and bath puff threaded onto Aluminium wire to create "scrunched" groupings; were added to finish the arrangement whilst hiding the mechanics.

P32

Midelino/ Midollino sticks are normally sold in bundles of 150 and are extremely versatile as they are pliable and therefore very useful to construct structures.

1/ Tape 4 x 50cm x 1.8mm black stub wires with a suitable coloured florist tape. Bend 1 taped wire to measure 5cms, bend at an angle to start to form a hexagon shape before measuring 10cms and then bend, repeat 3 more times and then bend to finish with a 5cms length at the end. Cut a second taped 1.8mm wire to create 2 x 10cm sides of the hexagon and tape to create a full hexagon shape.

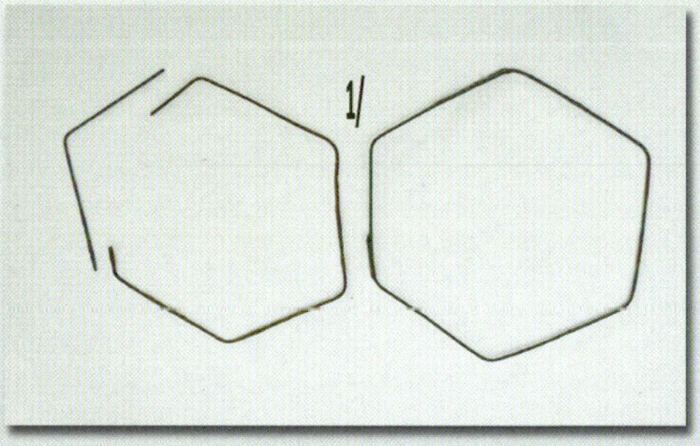

2/ Take a third taped 1.8mm wire and lay against one side of the hexagon so the top of the wire is at the top of a hexagonal side and securely tape to form a “leg”. Take the 4th taped 1.8mm wire and bend the tip 5cms at a 90 degree angle and secure to the adjacent hexagonal side to create a second, slightly longer neighbouring “leg”.

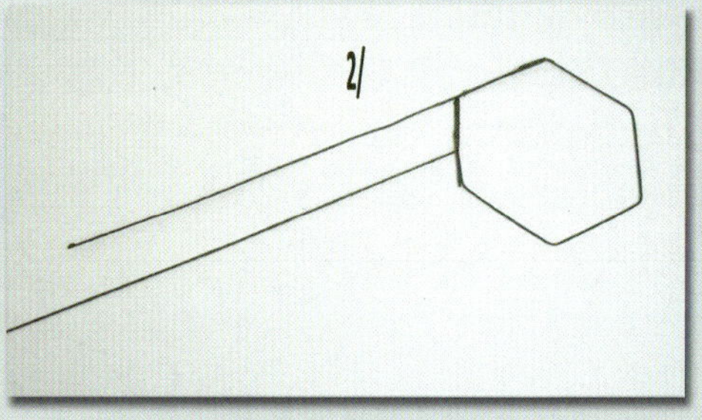

3/ Using 30 x 60cms Midelino sticks, make 6 x 5 stick bundles, bound together neatly with colour coordinated wire. Ensure you have a 20cm length of wire extending from each end. You may find you have 80cm Midollino from another manufacturer.

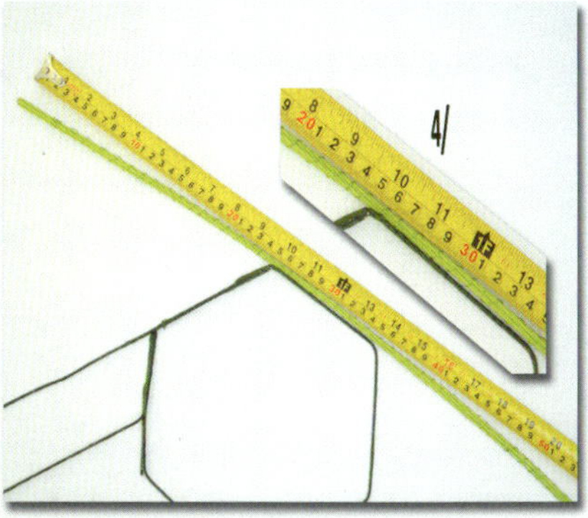

4/ Taking the wire mechanic, place one wired bundle up against a hexagonal side so the bundle extending from the 10cm side is of equal distance in length- i.e. 25cms. If you have 80cm long Midollino make sure the lengths are 35cms either side of the 10cms hexagon side you are working with.

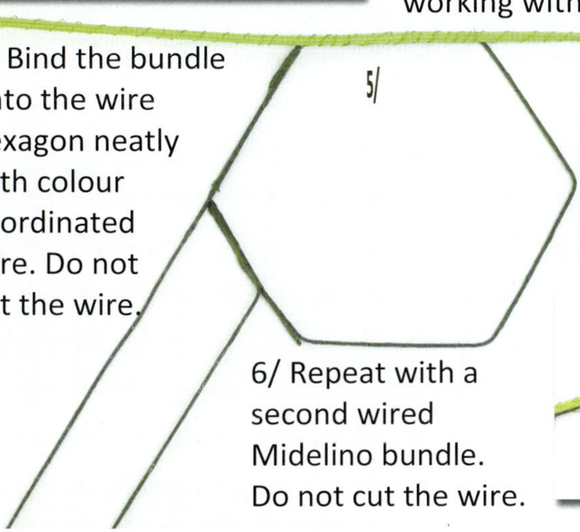

5/ Bind the bundle onto the wire hexagon neatly with colour coordinated wire. Do not cut the wire.

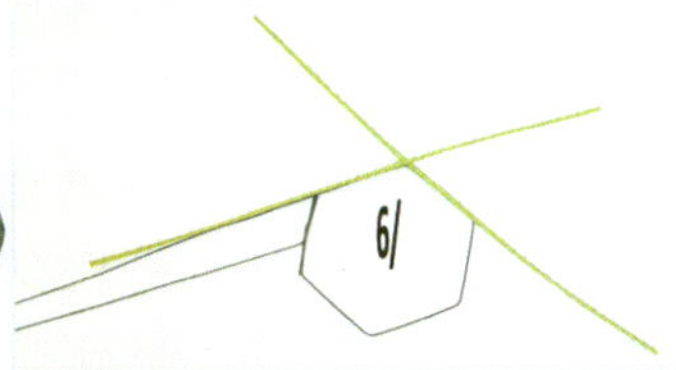

6/ Repeat with a second wired Midelino bundle. Do not cut the wire.

7/ Repeat measuring and attaching the remaining 4 wired Midelino bundles; cut the wire. Commence wiring the extended bundles at the tips to form a six pointed star with the extending 20cm wire lengths.

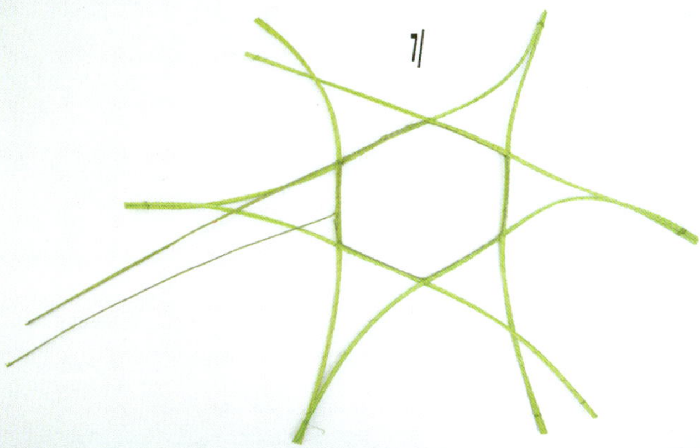

P34

8/ Finish by decorating the star points with soft, scrunched, bullion wire decoration and Aluminium wire swirls.

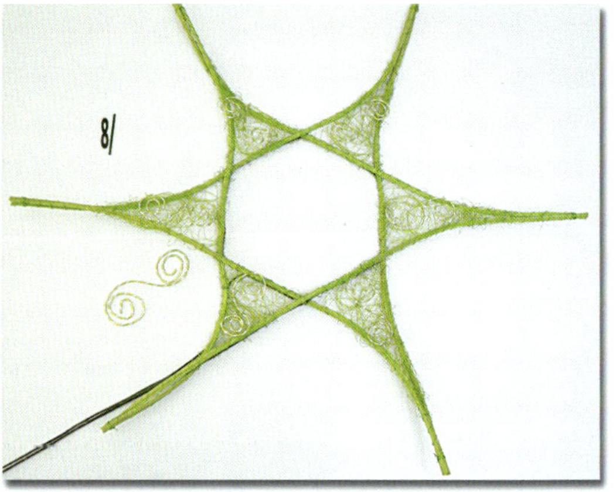

9/ To make the arrangement, it is easier to tie the tall placements to the star framework for support and control.
Start by tying the foliage backbone to the star strategically.

10/ Continue to arrange the placements, stems spiralling, just as you would arrange them in floral foam.
Make sure the stems which will be in the vase are clear of thorns and leaves. Try not to hide the centre enclosed space of the star.

11/ Tie to secure the hand tied placements and legs of the star to stay in position.

12/ Measure and cut the stems to rest on the base of the vase. Remove any leaves you feel hide the star's enclosed space.

Midelino Star

P36

Finish arranging the design. Precision cut the stems. You will find that the arranged materials will be supported by the spiralled stems of the hand tied for control and anchorage.

By making this design firstly as a hand tied and completed as an arrangement you will bc able to achieve necessary profile.

Midelino Star

This Festive wall hanger uses 60cm lengths of Black Midelino.

The two layered wire flower is made with an Aluminium wire outer framework for each petal, in filled with scrunched bullion wire bound onto the framework. Glass beads were threaded individually onto metallic wire to make 'stamens'.
The bead stamens and individual petals were assembled to form a flower, wired securely to hold into position before the flower was wired onto the star for effect.

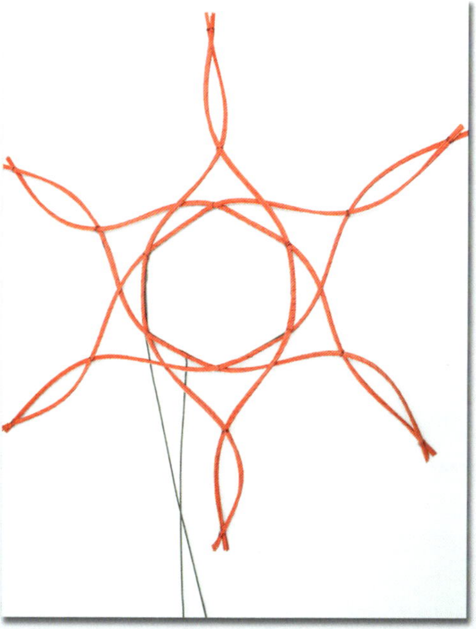

This elaborate star is made from 80cm lengths of Midollino.

The construction of which is the same as previously described until you create the star points.

Join 2 bundles of Midollino as before to make a point and secure with wire. Then cross over the same 2 bundles to make an "eye" shape and bind together circa 8cms away from a hexagon point. This creates a star with greater visual movement.

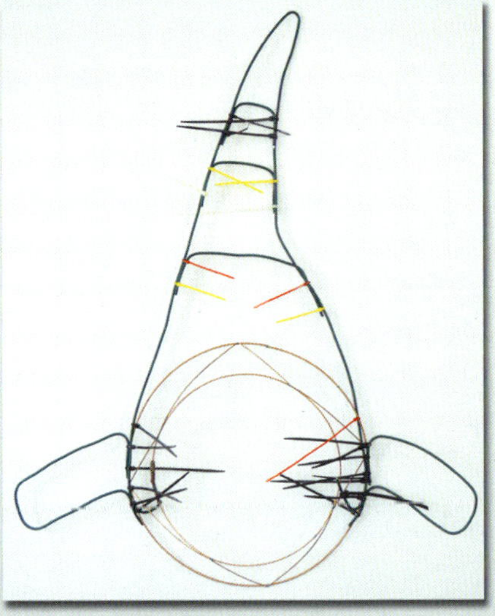

What better way to welcome your visitors than to have a Santa Welcome Wreath to make people smile.

The main framework is made from a raised wire 31cm (12 inch) ring.

To make the arms cut 2 lengths of green coated strong garden wire each measuring 50cms in length. Measure 5cms and bend to echo the outside curve of the wire ring before bending at a right angle to start to construct the arm. Create a slight curve measuring 18cms before bending at a right angle and then measure 5cms and then bend at a right angle and measure 17cms and then bend the remaining 5cms of wire to again echo the curve of the outer wire ring. Repeat so you have 2 curved arms and strategically attach with cable ties and pot tape securely.

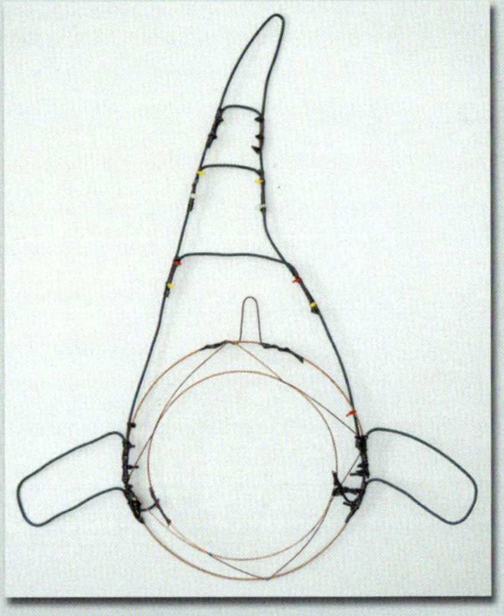

For Santa's hat measure 80cms of green coated strong garden wire and bend the wire to create a curved hat. Secure with cable ties and pot tape to the raised wire ring.

To strengthen the hat cut 3 more lengths of garden wire measuring: 10cms, 20cms and 25cms. Bend each end to echo the wire outline of the hat and secure with cable ties.

Make a wire loop for hanging at the top of the outer 31cm raised ring and secure with pot tape.

Cut off the residue cable ties.

Santa Welcome Wreath

1/ Moss the 31cm raised wire ring, arms and two thirds of the hat using the “sausage technique” as described on pages 16-17. Trim neatly.

2/ Moss a 20 cm raised wire ring again using the “sausage” technique. Do not trim. Dismantle a second 20cm raised wire ring so that the inner ring and struts are remaining.

3/ Cut a 25cm (10 inch) square of copper wire mesh and mould it around the ring. Secure the ring with its struts and hair pin wires made of 10cm lengths of 1.00mm green coated wire.

4/ Make a round dense domed disc shape of teased moss to cover the copper mesh and bind to secure with green jute string.

5/ Cut another piece of copper wire mesh to infill the remaining part of the hat. Mould to secure.

6/ Make bespoke size “sausages” to densely fill the hat and bind to secure, making sure you do not cover the hanging loop when binding. Tie the jute string to cast off and trim as appropriate.

7/ Cut the Picea pungens (Blue Pine) into 3 different length piles. Cut the larger lengths to circa 20 x 18cm (7 inch) "hand sized" bushy tips, then cut around 25 x 14cm (5 ½ inch) " 3 pronged" tips and then 30 x 6cm (3 inch) tips. You will need 3 or 4 branches dependent upon their size.

8/ Using the double leg mount method of wiring, use 30cm x 1.00mm Green Lacquered stub wires cut in half and wire up a quantity of the prepared cut Blue Pine. If you don't want to wire up the Blue Pine you can pin the Blue Pine on with mossing pins or equivalent.

9/ To edge and base the moss, work with the underside of the Pine facing upwards, insert the legs of the double leg mount in the direction you wish the tips of the blue pine to be. Push the wires right in, at an acute diagonal angle, until the stem ends touch the moss.

10/ Then bend the Blue Pine over so it is facing upwards with the tips facing outwards. This method ensures the Blue Pine will not fall out as the moss dries and shrinks or the wreath moves.

Santa Welcome Wreath

Edge and base, in close order, the mossed hat, arms and 2 raised wire rings with the blue pine. The tips always pointing outwards for effect. Always start from the outside edge and work inwards to create even basing. You will need to select the appropriate size of blue pine to achieve the definition required. I used single tips for the edging of the arms to ensure I achieved a clear outline shape. The hat and body were edged with 3 pronged tips and "hand sized" tips were used for the inner body and hat.

11/ Cut out a beard shape using white waterproof packing material and pin to secure into position. Select an 8cm Styropor Solid Sphere for the nose.

Cover the Styropor Solid Sphere with coloured sisal and wire into position.

12/ To make the beard, undo 2 x white bath puffs and scrunch and hold into position before pinning with mossing pins for even coverage.

Trim Santa's hat and make cuffs with felt pinned into position. Make 2 moss feet attached to flat aluminium wire springs and insert to form wobbly legs. Decorate as appropriate with felt trim and baubles on wires.

Santa Welcome Wreath

P43

Finish by making a pair of glasses using flat aluminium wire and add bauble eyes. A little grouping of baubles and aluminium wire were added at the top of his hat to create unity.

Red Star Vase

P44

1/ To make the stem of the vase, use 5 x 50cm x 1.8mm black stub wires. Measure 13 cms up from the base of the bundled wires and bind with metallic wire, to band in close order 8cms down leaving 5cms of the wire visible.
Do not cut the wire.

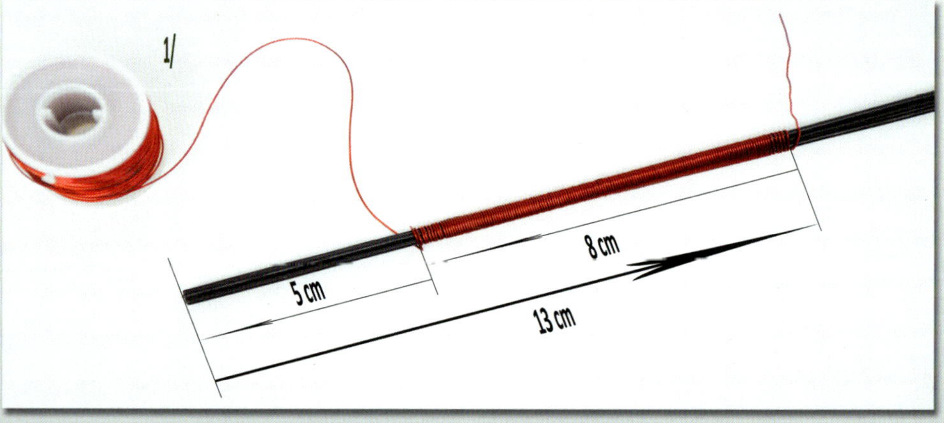

2/ Splay out the 1.8mm 5cm stub wires at a 90 degree angle, equidistant apart, to form the foot of the vase.

3/ Commence the wire weave technique, in close, tight order, to secure the 1.80mm stub wires into position for circa 1cm.
Do not cut the wire.

4/ Change the wiring technique to make a flat base by binding over each splayed 1.80mm wire to form a "cob web" look.

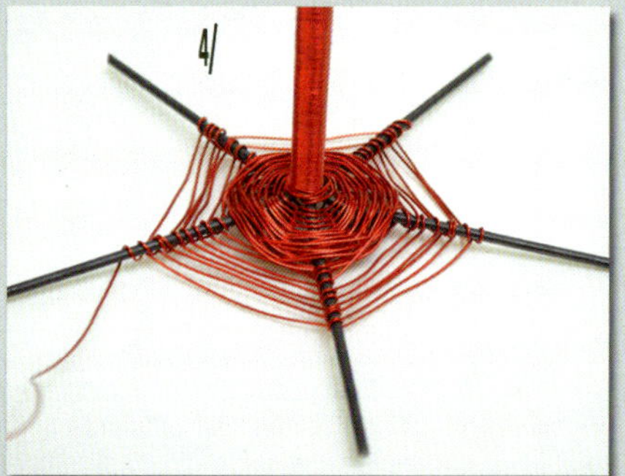

Red Star Vase

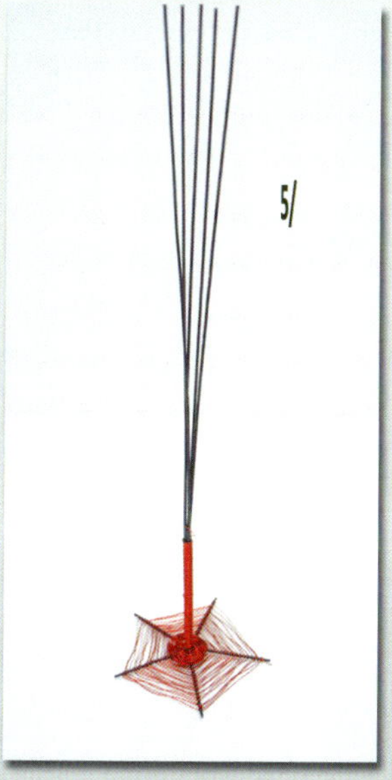

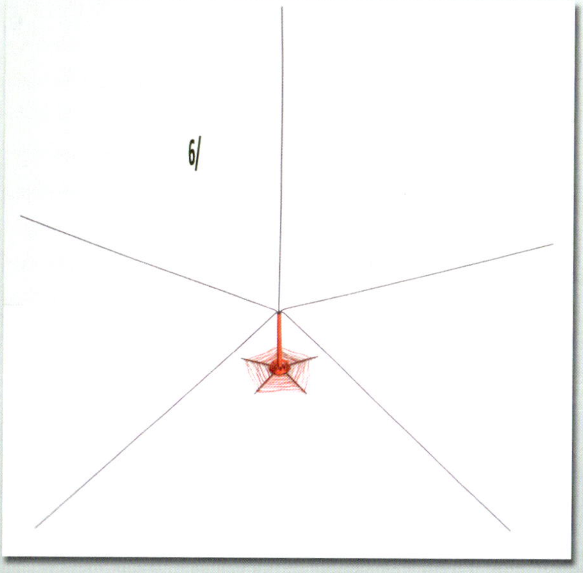

5/ When you are half a centimetre away from the stub wire tips stop "cob web" wiring. Cut the wire. Leaving the tip free of wire is to enable a bead to be glued on to aid the finished appearance.

6/ Bend the 1.80mm wires at the top of the vase stem at a 90 degree angle.

7/ Select a lightweight vase/ candle holder. Place the base of the vase to rest on the vase stem, in the middle, and carefully bend mould the wires to curve to support the vase.

Red Star Vase

P46

8/ Make your 10cm sided star using the alternate chain link technique on page 14.

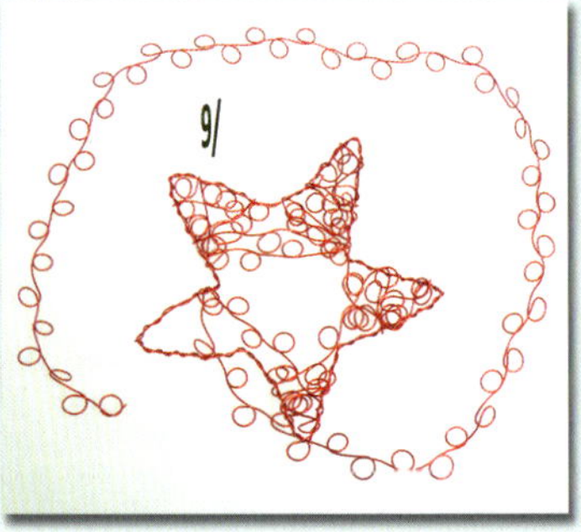

9/ Commence wrapping the alternate chain link around a star point until softly covered and then lead the chain across to a different star point and repeat. Complete by using all the alternate chain to create a visually balanced covered star.

10/ Carefully thread the stub wires through the star points. It is not an easy process. If you find it too difficult cut the stub wires shorter – yet long enough to support the star into position.

11/ Complete the Red Star Vase by hot gluing a bead onto each stub wire end.

To finish, add a choice flower and complementary foliage.

This Red Star Vase showcases a woven Liriope muscari (China Grass) "flower" with Hedera and Pinus to aid textural contrast.

P48

1/ Using a 100cm externally plaited palm, create a ribbon bow at the tip do not cut the ribbon. * Select a Rose and weave the stem through the fronds to anchor the rose into position. If you have not externally plaited before, you will find the complete instructions in my book "How to.. Go Greener Flower Arranging - Leaf Manipulation and Bark and Cone Structures - Volume 1" pages 52 to 54.

2/ Add a second Rose and a few glittered stems, by weaving them through the fronds to aid stability and thread the ribbon through the fronds to also lightly stitch the placements into position.

3/ Continue to arrange 3 more roses and glittered stems for effect. Where possible weave the stems through and use the ribbon to thread stitch your placements into position. Tie the stems together with string and disguise with 12mm green pot tape.

Plaited Palm Vertical Hand Tied with Threading

Place the hand tied into your selected vase.

Arrange 5 looped Aspidistra to create a collar and add 3 grouped baubles glued onto sticks.

Finish by adding a few more glittered stems to create unity throughout the design.

How to " Externally Plait" pages 52 to 54

Knotted and Looptubed Aspidistra ...

P50

A slim rectangular vase houses a mechanic made from knotted and looptubed Aspidistra with the addition of a 14cm length of 40mm diameter PVC push fit waste pipe, the manipulated Aspidistra rests on the vase with the Aspidistra knot stems acting as stilts resting on the vase's base.

Two knotted Aspidistra were placed close next to each other and secured with pot tape. Before placing the other 2, close together, opposite the first 2 and secured at the top and bottom of the pipe.

To make a looptubed Aspidistra, fold the leaf, without creasing, where the midrib vein becomes pliable and staple.

Manipulate the leaf to make a tube which overlaps the stapled leaf and staple into position either side of the midrib vein.

Knotted and Looptubed Aspidistra ...

Commence arranging the design through the waste pipe and once full continue to arrange through the knots and gaps.

The Calla lilies can be arranged through the Aspidistra knots and looptubes for effect.

Mechanic with Waste Pipe Mechanic

Circular Fir Cone Collar Using the Chain Twist Technique

P54

To make a circular fir cone collar, use the same rustic wire chain twist technique on pages 20-21. Instead of stitching baubles into position, fir cones can be screwed into each hole.

Make sure the bottom scales of each fir cone are secured firmly between the rustic wires.

Circular Fir Cone Collar Using the Chain Twist Technique

To make a willow roll container. Cut the willow roll to size to fit around a coffee jar and secure with natural paper covered wire.

Make a mesh of paper covered wire where the roll is wire stitched together at one end to enable the jar to sit inside the willow roll.

Open up the rustic wire spokes of the fir cone collar. This will enable materials to be arranged through for support and anchorage. Place the fir cone collar into the jar, decorated with the willow roll and wire up additional cones ready to include in your design.

Circular Fir Cone Collar Using the Chain Twist Technique

P56

As winter foliage is so attractive, I thought I would make an all round table design showcasing additional leaf manipulation techniques; the Aspidistra "rose" with both variegated and green leaves, a woven Liriope muscari (China Grass) "Rose" and braiding with the help of a few dried Eryngiums and a host of festive foliage loveliness.

Circular Fir Cone Collar Using the Chain Twist Technique

P57

Candle Holder Container

P58

Having made the red star container...... I had a mad moment and thought what if?

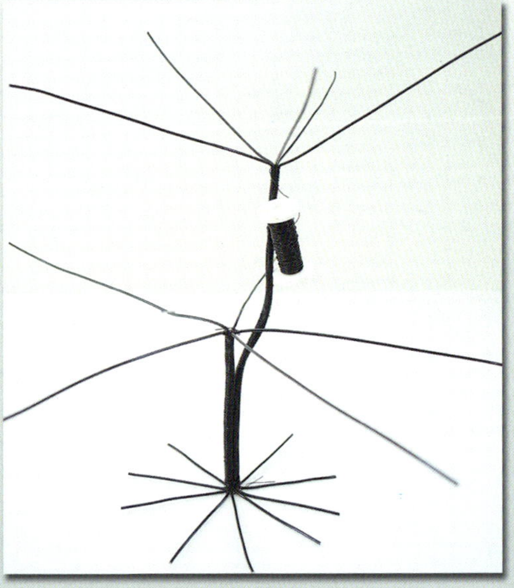

Using the same techniques as described when making the red star container, I commenced making the 2 vase stems using 5 x 50cm x 1.8mm black stub wires for each stem. The stems are of different lengths to enable the candle holders to have sufficient space within the structure without clashing and the taller wire was curved for greater interest.

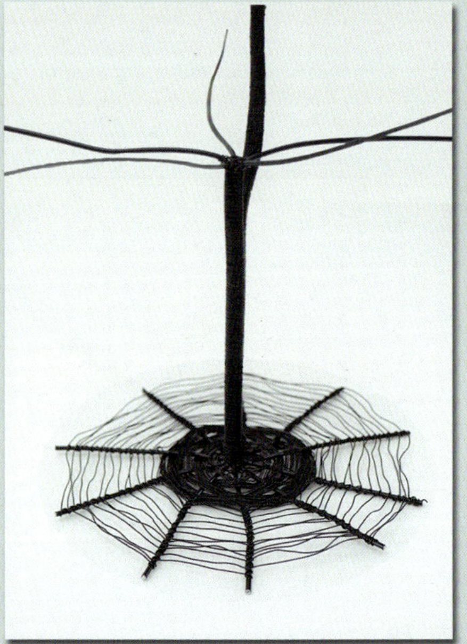

I then bent the base wires to form the foot so that they became as one and splayed out, equidistant apart.

Next, I used the wire weave wiring technique and the "cob web" technique before gluing a bead on to the end of each wire to complete the base.

To support my 2 candle holders, in turn, the 1.8mm wires, above the bound 'stems' were carefully bent around each candle holder.

Candle Holder Container

For decorative purposes the residue wires were bent to make loops and the foot was secured onto a silver sprayed wood slice by drilling small holes and attaching with metallic wire.

 Designing a diamond shaped table arrangement constructed without floral foam has been a test.
I do hope you agree this is the answer.

1/ Select a shallow dish which has low sides but able to hold sufficient water. I have used a 30cm (12 inch) x 15cms (6 inch) rectangular glass dish, the sides of which are 4cms (1½ inch) in height.

1/

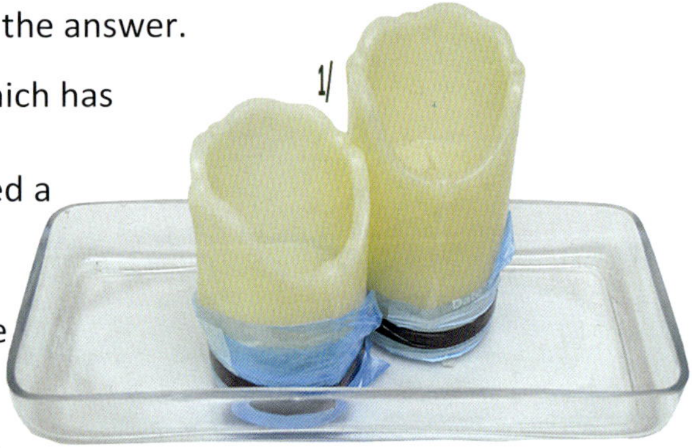

I have used 2 faux candles, to avoid any fire risk issues, the bottoms of which have been placed into plastic bags, secured with pot tape, for protection.

2/ Using 7.5 metres of aluminium wire, I measured 3.75m to find the middle of the wire and used the chain twist technique (see pages 20-21) around each faux candle as a means of anchoring them into the dish. Do not cut the wire.

The residue lengths of wire were then made into 2 x alternate chain links using the technique as described on pages 14-15.

2/

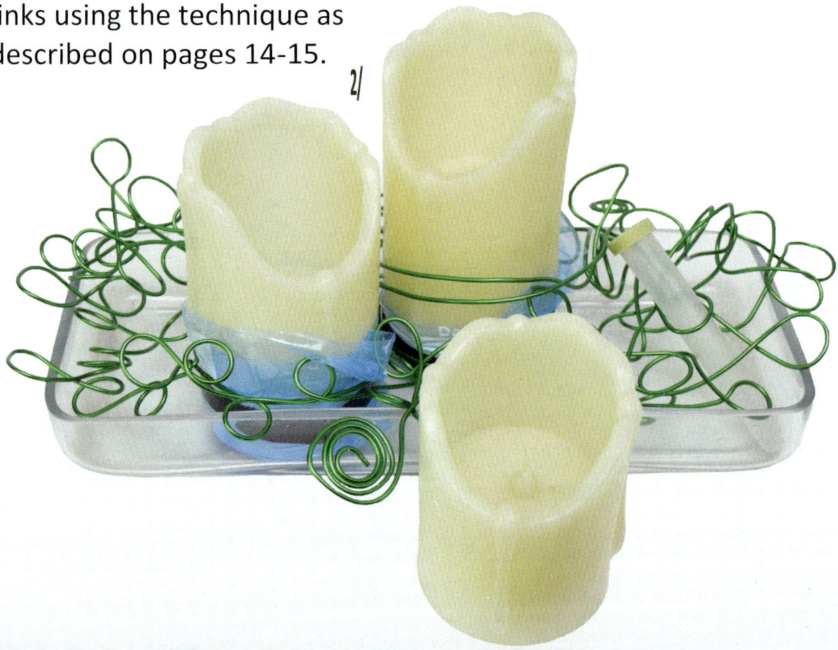

Position the candles in the dish, anchored by the Aluminium chain twist mechanic and then position the lengths of alternate chain links so they evenly fill the dish over 2/3 layers, making sure some chain link circles are adjacent to the sides of the dish. To help hold the alternate chain link chains into position, use strategic elastic bands around the dish/chains both width wise and length wise. Add sufficient water.

I added a third candle to sit adjacent to the dish for effect. Commence arranging the outline shape. Try and use slightly curved foliage to be able to hide the sides of the dish whilst ensuring the stems are supported by the aluminium wire chain and are in water.

You can use the wire to clamp the longer stems into position.

Finish the design as required ensuring it is no larger than one third the size of the table and as low as 20cms for the mechanics to support, control and anchor your materials into position.

I thought I would lift the arrangement up so that you can see that it doesn't fall apart

and you can see the water level and the curved stems.

Fabric Ribbon Mesh Flower

P64

I always have a range of handmade "flowers" available in case I need that extra bit of colour to fulfil my design requirements.

I have used, 5cm width, fabric mesh ribbon and cut 1 x 1 metre length and 5 x 25cms lengths.

1/ To make the flowers centre. Take the 1 metre length of ribbon, hold it at the end and fold it over at a 90 degree angle. Do not crease.

2/ Begin to twist the ribbon towards you.

3/ Then fold the ribbon away from you.

4/ And continue twisting the same way to increase the size of the flower's centre.

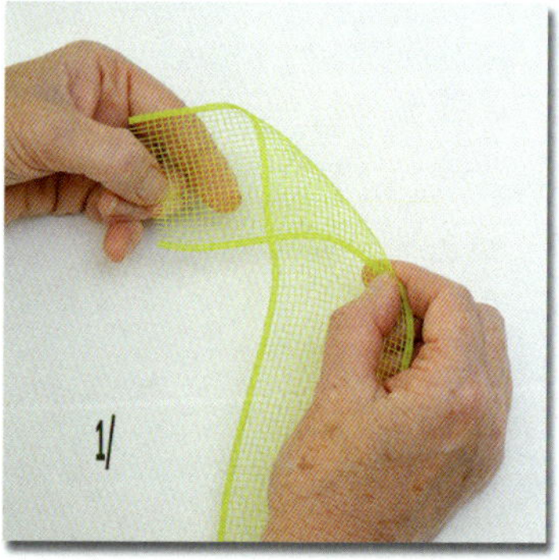

5/ Continue folding and twisting, ensuring you keep the top level for effect.

6/ Bind to secure into position with metallic wire. Do not cut the wire.

7/ Take one piece of the 25cm ribbon and make a petal loop. Scrunch the ends.

8/ Position to form a 'petal' and bind to secure.
Do not cut the wire.

9/ Continue using each 25cm length of ribbon mesh to make petal loops and strategically bind to secure.

10/ Position the loops to be at slightly different angles to aid greater interest.

11/ Finish by binding with the wire downwards to create a, neat, firm, "stem" base. Cut the wire and cut the mesh ribbon to create a neat edge.

12/ A Rhapis excelsa (Finger palm) leaf has been manipulated to make alternate rolls secured with double sided tape.

40 Blades of Liriope gigantea (Lily Grass) were used to make the plaited heart. A lovely structure which can be dried and spray painted as evidenced in the base placement.

Fabric Ribbon Mesh Flower

This elegant arrangement showcases the mesh flowers to perfection in this slim lily vase.

How to: "Rhapis Palm roll" page 37.
How to: "Plait China Grass Heart" pages 26 to 27

Sisal Container

P68

This Winter design was made from a recycled 500ml water bottle and some purple sisal sheeting to create a textural container. A 30cm square of sisal sheeting was cut, with a strategic circular hole for the water bottle. The sisal sheet was manipulated to form a tube with a 3cm (1 inch) overlap secured by staples. The hole was big enough to house a recycled, cut down, plastic water bottle, which was also covered in the same sisal sheeting.

A few additional circles were cut out for design effect.

A small transparent aluminium ball was made to be inserted into the cut down bottle as the mechanic.

Hellebores, Erica (Heather) and Skimmia japonica were then arranged to create this simple Winter design.

Knotted Aspidistra

P70

Clean both sides of an Aspidistra elatior leaf with a wet wipe to remove any residue.

Cut lengthwise the leaf blade equally in half until you feel the midrib vein (central vein) is too woody to bend. You will find the midrib vein is not central so one half of the leaf will have the midrib vein present.

Hold the leaf upright, underside facing you, so that the stiff half is erect and the floppy half flows away from you.

Knotted Aspidistra

Whilst holding the stem in one hand, hold the tip of the stiff half leaf and bring towards you

before manoeuvring it so it goes underneath the floppy leaf and is eventually positioned to be at right angles to the stem

to make a loop that has a hole through which two fingers can pass.

Insert the tip half way up through the loop and pull the tip through the hole to be sufficiently long

You will need to make sure the floppy half leaf is not twisted. Place 2 fingers through what looks like the "knot of a tie" to loosen it sufficiently so that you can insert the tip of the floppy half up through the "tie knot".

in order that you can bring the tip downwards and towards you; to the leaf base to form what looks like a slightly puffed arrow head. Constantly hold in position and turn the leaf structure round to the other side.

Knotted Aspidistra

P73

Catch hold of it's tip and ease it up through the "tie knot" until the length is long enough to be brought down to the leaf base towards you; in order to make a puffed shape. Secure the manipulated knot structure with paper covered wire.

Grouped Aspidistra knots can be incorporated in a design for distinction or can be used as a mechanic. Flower stems can be threaded through the knots which hold them into position.

From the Author

The designing of this “How to” Foam Free, Festive/ Winter Floral Design Book has made me try to replicate the design styles we have enjoyed when using floral foam by using and designing alternative mechanics. I wanted to explore ways of showcasing less flowers and foliage in Festive Floral designs which still achieve distinction.

I also wanted to incorporate a host of different leaf manipulation techniques which again helps to create the “wow” factor.
I truly believe Aluminium wire is the key to alternative mechanics as it can be reused time and time again with a little help of being cleaned with an anti bacterial agent. Such a versatile material, lightweight and pliable which does not always need to be hidden as it can also be an intricate part of a design.

I also have found that arranging the taller placements as a hand tied, secured with string and pot tape, before placing in a vase is an easy way of keeping the taller materials controlled, prior to arranging the remainder of the design and achieving the profile necessary for a well anchored and executed design.

I do hope that you are happy with the designs I have shared with you.

Festive Greetings.

P75

Index

Index

Further Reading - Page 78
www.gillmcgregor.com/books

Further Reading

P78

'50 Techniques Used in Contemporary Floral Designs' - Seventy different floral designs of distinction illustrate the 50 Techniques listed in alphabetical order for easy reference.
ISBN 978-0-9929332-0-3

'How to.. Contemporary Floral Design Wire Manipulation' Over 140 photographs support more than 40 different contemporary floral designs with concise construction methods.
ISBN 978-0-9929332-1-0

'How to.. Make Living Vases, Screens & Structures for Contemporary Floral Designs.' Over 160 photographs explaining how to make over 50 living vases, screens or structures. ISBN 978-0-9929332-3-4

How to.. Apply The Elements & Principles of Floral Design 'My Little Black Book' This book steps you through each Element of Design and how they each need to satisfy the Principles of Design - supported with over 150 different floral designs - and 240 different images - to ***Inspire!*** ISBN 978-0-9929332-4-1

How to.. Go Greener Flower Arranging: Leaf Manipulation & Bark and Cone Structures - Volume 1
The manipulation of plant material has revolutionised floral design - Over 250 full colour images.
ISBN 978-0-9929332-6-5

How to.. Go Greener Floral Foam Free - Volume 1
Enables the reader to create 20 different floral designs using Alternative Mechanics instead of Floral Foam.
ISBN 978-0-9929332-7-2

How to.. Alternative Mechanics for Foam Free Floral Designs, Volume 2 Enables the reader to create a further range of different floral designs using new, exciting, Alternative Mechanics. 200 Full colour photographs, with supporting narrative text, showing the elegance of 'foam free' flower arranging.
ISBN 978-0-9929332-8-9